A MOTHER'S LOVE

a heartfelt journey

A MOTHER'S LOVE

a heartfelt journey

WRITTEN BY
RUTH HOVSEPIAN

To all the mothers.

A NOTE FROM RUTH

You are a treasured daughter in God's Kingdom and blessed and chosen by Him to be a mother. I, too, am a mother and have experienced the kind of love only shared between a mother and her children. While you may be blessed with a different framework, I am blessed with two daughters and one son.

This book celebrates the profound love that exists between mothers and their children. Through this heartfelt poem and beautiful illustrations, I have attempted to capture the essence of a mother's unwavering bond with her child. While mere words cannot fully explain this bond, I pray this book fills your heart with the essence of the love you have created and nurtured within your child.

Please feel honored, deeply loved, and cherished that your son or daughter gifted you the words within these pages. You are their anchor of love on this earth, the one they look to when their world has come undone. You've tended to every hurt, helped correct every wrong, and been their most avid cheerleader. The only One Who has done more for your child is their Creator, our Lord, Who's designed you to be the caretaker here. So, relish all the sentiments this book holds, and be blessed as you read every word.

Whether you are a mother, a mother-to-be, a grandmother, or someone who has embraced the role of a nurturing figure, may this book touch your soul and resonate with the eternal connection born out of love.

Join me now as we explore the tender moments, cherish the memories, and illuminate the everlasting connection that resides in a mother's heart, a connection that transcends time.

Ruth Hovsepian

To:

From:

In your warm embrace, love's gentle tide,
A bond unbreakable, always by my side.

Your caring touch, a soothing balm,
In your arms, I am forever calm.

A beacon of strength, a guiding light,
Through life's storms, you hold me tight.

Your selfless love, like a gentle breeze,
Whispering words that put my heart at ease.

With every sacrifice, you make me see,
The depth of a mother's love is the key.

Your nurturing spirit, a guiding force,
Shaping my path with unwavering course.

On this day, I celebrate you,
A mother's love, pure and true.

Thank you, dear mom, for all you do,
Forever grateful, I am to you.

Through laughter and tears, you're always there,
A constant presence, showing me, you care.

You wipe away my tears and fears,
And fill my days with joy and cheer.

In your eyes, I see strength and grace,
A reflection of love, on your face.

You lift me up when I am down,
A faithful protector, never wanting me to frown.

You teach me lessons, big and small,
Ready to catch me when I stumble and fall.

With your wisdom and direction, I do grow,
Blossoming into the best version you can know.

Your love a shield, protecting me,
From the storms that life may decree.

You wrap me in warmth, in a cozy embrace,
Creating a haven, a sacred space.

So, on this day, I honor you,
For who you are and all you do.

You are the heart and soul of our family,
A pillar of strength and unconditional love, living gracefully.

Thank you, dear mom, for being by my side,
For being my rock, my unchanging guide.

I treasure the moments we share together,
Grateful for you, now and forever.

WAYS TO
CONNECT

For more information, please visit Ruth's website, www.ruthhovsepian.com,
where you will find her podcast, blog, videos, speaking calendar, free resources,
and all her latest news and information.

To book Ruth to speak at your next event, please visit ruthhovsepian.com
or email info@ruthhovsepian.com for more details.

ALSO WRITTEN BY
RUTH HOVSEPIAN

100 DAYS OF PRAYER:
A journey into deeper intimacy with GOD

100 DAYS OF PRAYER:
Prayer Journal Edition

THE ULTIMATE CONVERSATION
Is that you, God?

PREPARE HIM ROOM
25 Devotionals Celebrating The Birth Of Jesus

WHAT THEY'RE SAYING

PREPARE HIM ROOM

Ruth's book is so well written to inspire and encourage you in the days leading up to Christmas Day. What an excellent tool for the serious Christian to prepare for a meaningful and heartfelt worship experience. —Edsel B., United States

THE ULTIMATE CONVERSATION

I'm enjoying reading about prayer as a reminder to turn to God, not only in the hard times, but also in the good times. We can worship God any time everywhere. A meaty concise revelation of the importance of prayer in the Christian's life with spiritual quotes from giants of faith like C.S. Lewis, St. Augustine and others. Scripture references are well quoted to help the reader understand faith in a God who is there for us, and who wants to have conversations with His people. —Pirkko, Canada

100 DAYS OF PRAYERS

I was given this book as a gift, and it has been a beautiful give to have received. Love the blending of personal life story along with sound biblical teaching leaving everyone with things to think about as we lean on God through prayer. Perfect for the person new to a prayer life and the seasoned Christion who already has a deep rich prayer life. The cover is inviting leaving the reader to want to go on this journey. —Teresa M., United States